EXPLORING THE ORIGINS OF THE UNIVERSE

Stuart A. Kallen

D1243390

Series Editor:
Arthur Upgren, Professor of Astronomy
Wesleyan University

Twenty-First Century Books

A Division of Henry Holt and Company
New York

Twenty-First Century Books
A division of Henry Holt and Company, Inc.
115 West 18th Street
New York, New York 10011

Henry Holt® and colophon are registered trademarks of Henry Holt and Company, Inc.
Publishers since 1866

©1997 by Blackbirch Graphics, Inc.
First Edition
5 4 3 2 1
Published in Canada by Fitzhenry & Whiteside Ltd.
195 Allstate Parkway, Markham, Ontario L3R 4T8

Printed in the United States of America on acid free paper ∞.

Created and produced in association with Blackbirch Graphics, Inc.

Photo Credits

Cover (background) and page 4: ©NASA; cover (inset): ©Jerry Lodriguss/Photo Researchers, Inc.; page 6: ©Chris Bjornberg/Science Source/Photo Researchers, Inc.; page 9: ©1996 North Wind Pictures; pages 10, 16: ©Scala/Art Resource, NY; pages 11, 14, 19: North Wind Picture Archives; page 21: ©Julian Baum/Science Photo Library/Photo Researchers, Inc.; pages 22, 37, 50: AP/Wide World Photos; page 27: National Archives; page 34: ©Tony Craddock/Science Photo Library/Photo Researchers, Inc.; page 38: ©David A. Hardy/Science Photo Library/Photo Researchers, Inc.; page 41: ArSciMed/Science Photo Library/Photo Researchers, Inc.; page 47: ©Dr. Rob Stepney/Science Photo Library/Photo Researchers, Inc.; page 48: Max-Planck-Institut fur Physik und Astrophysik/Science Photo Library/Photo Researchers, Inc.; page 52: ©Science Photo Library/Photo Researchers, Inc.; pages 53, 57: ©Mehau Kulyk/Science Photo Library/Photo Researchers, Inc.; page 54: ©Fermi National Accelerator Laboratory/Photo Researchers, Inc.
Artwork by Blackbirch Graphics, Inc.

Library of Congress Cataloging-in-Publication Data

Kallen, Stuart A., 1955–
    Exploring the origins of the universe / Stuart A. Kallen.
       p.   cm. — (Secrets of space)
    Includes bibliographical references and index.
    Summary: Discusses various beliefs about the origin and nature of the universe and the studies of such scientists as Copernicus, Galileo, Kepler, and Einstein, who have advanced our understanding of the universe.
    ISBN 0-8050-4478-7
    1. Astronomy—History—Juvenile literature. 2. Cosmology—Juvenile literature. 3. Astronomers—Biography—Juvenile literature. 4. Physicists—Biography—Juvenile literature. [1. Cosmology. 2. Astronomers. 3. Physicists.] I. Title. II. Series.
QB46.K35   1997
523—dc21
                                                       96-37366
                                                        CIP
                                                        AC

TABLE OF CONTENTS

INTRODUCTION

Humans have always been fascinated by space, but it has been only since the 1950s that technology has allowed us to actually travel beyond our Earth's atmosphere to explore the universe. What riches of knowledge this space exploration has brought us! All of the planets except Pluto have been mapped extensively, if not completely. Among the planets, only Pluto has not been visited by a space probe, and that will likely change soon. Men have walked on the Moon, and many of the satellites of Jupiter, Saturn, Uranus, and even Neptune have been investigated in detail.

We have learned the precise composition of the Sun and the atmospheres of the planets. We know more about comets, meteors, and asteroids than ever before. And many scientists now think there may be other forms of life in our galaxy and beyond.

In the *Secrets of Space* series, we journey through the wondrous world of space: our solar system, our galaxy, and our universe. It is a world seemingly without end, a world of endless fascination.

—Arthur Upgren
Professor of Astronomy
Wesleyan University

People have gazed into the night skies for centuries, wondering about our place among the stars.

CHAPTER 1

THE ORIGINS OF THE UNIVERSE

The twinkling night sky is full of mystery. Standing beneath the starry sky, our day-to-day problems often seem to fade into the darkness. We stare up at the same stars our distant ancestors gazed upon ages ago. The heavens seem to be eternally constant, even though we know Earth is always changing.

The stars and galaxies have long presented us with riddles. Some of those riddles we may never answer. But as long as humans have walked on Earth, they have pondered the same questions. Where did we come from? How long have we been here? What is our place among the stars? How did the universe, or cosmos, begin?

Many Cultures, Many Beliefs

Although these questions may seem impossible to answer, that has not stopped us from trying. Today, most scientists believe the universe was created with one "big bang," and that it continues to evolve in a gradual expansion. But ancient peoples had different beliefs.

Powerful telescopes, computers, satellites, and other tools help us to search for clues to the beginning of the universe. But long ago, people could only use the naked eye to observe the skies. They saw lightning shoot from the sky and start fires. Many believed that lightning came from the stars or the Sun. That led them to think that powerful gods and goddesses lived in the sky. Almost every culture has myths, legends, and stories about how the universe was created.

The Hindus, for example, believe in Brahma—a four-headed god who created both the universe and humanity. When Brahma sleeps, the universe is destroyed—nothing exists. When Brahma awakens, the universe—and everything in it—is created anew. The Hindus believe that this cycle of destruction and creation continues on for eternity.

The ancient Egyptians worshipped the Sun God Re (or Ra) as the creator of the universe. Re was believed to give birth to himself at the beginning of time. But Re was lonely and decided to create the world. Re spit, and from his spit was formed the air—named Shu—and moisture—named Tefnut. Shu and Tefnut had children—Geb, the Earth God, and Nut, the Sky Goddess. Humans were formed from Re's tears. Re knit together the mountains and made animals, the heavens, and Earth.

The ancient Chinese also have a story of how the universe was created. It is known as the Cosmic Egg. Like many ancient creation stories, there are several different versions, but the basic themes in each are similar. The story of the Cosmic Egg begins with the two opposite forces of the universe—yin and yang. Yin is the power of shadow and darkness. Yang is the power of light and sunshine. Yin and yang had a child called P'an-ku—or Pan Gu. The ancient Chinese believed that it was Pan Gu who created the universe.

Islamic people believe the Koran—the Holy Book of Islam—was dictated by the angel Gabriel to the prophet Mohammed in the seventh century. The Koran says:

> *It is God who hath given you the Earth as a sure*
> *foundation, and over it built up the heavens, and*
> *formed you, and made your forms beautiful…*

The Jewish and Christian religions tell the story of one god who created the universe in six days. This story is written in the Holy Bible.

A painting from an Egyptian mummy case shows Shu (at right), Nut (with stars), and Geb (outstretched at bottom).

The Judeo-Christian story of the creation of the universe was depicted in several famous paintings by Italian artist Michelangelo. In this painting, God creates the planets and stars.

Star Gazers and New Discoveries

For thousands of years, human beings viewed creation as a gift from an all-knowing god or goddess in the sky. But as philosophers and scientists made new discoveries, some myths, legends, and theories were questioned.

As scientific and religious beliefs clashed, people had to modify their thinking. Beliefs about the universe began to change significantly when a new culture arose in Greece.

Greek thinkers proposed that Earth floated freely in space. They guessed the size of the Sun and Moon. Around 550 B.C., a mathematician named Pythagoras stated that Earth was round and planets moved through the sky on separate paths. In the second century A.D., an astronomer named Ptolemy said that

Earth was a solid body around which the Sun, Moon, planets, and stars revolved. This was known as the Ptolemaic, or geocentric (Earth-centered), theory.

Greek culture blossomed, off and on, for 800 years. Greek ideas spread to other parts of the world. In Egypt, great libraries were built. Ten large research halls were filled with half a million handwritten books. The libraries contained the writings of Greek and Egyptian astronomers along with books about medicine, physics, and math. New ways of looking at nature were developed. Scientific ideas flowed freely. Knowledge was respected.

Unfortunately, many people feared this new knowledge. The Roman Catholic Church, for example, did not accept many of the new Greek and Egyptian ideas. The Catholic Church used its enormous power over the mass population, and its doctrine overtook all others. During a period now known as the Dark Ages, many of the great discoveries of the Egyptian and Greek philosophers were lost or forgotten. The Catholic Church supported the old theories of Ptolemy—that Earth was the center of the universe. To question this theory was punishable by death. Scientific learning and discovery ground to a halt in Europe until the end of the Middle Ages in the fourteenth century.

Knowledge and ideas flourished in the great libraries of ancient Egypt.

Copernicus Revolutionizes Science

When the Renaissance started in the fourteenth century, a new era of scientific thought began with it. The invention of the printing press allowed new ideas to be widely spread. Old, firmly held beliefs were brought into question. And in 1543, the publication of the work of astronomer Nicolaus Copernicus caused a scientific revolution.

As a young man, Copernicus studied the works of the ancient Greeks. He was convinced that the movement of the heavens could only make sense if the Sun, and not Earth, was motionless. Copernicus observed that the further a planet was away from the Sun, the longer it took to orbit it. Mercury was closest to the Sun and only took 88 days to go completely around it. But Saturn, the farthest-known planet from the Sun at that time, took 30 years to make its journey. Earth, he theorized, was simply another one of the planets and he calculated that it took 365 days to orbit the Sun. (This calculation agreed with that of the ancient Egyptians who had developed a calendar almost 4,500 years earlier!)

Copernicus reasoned that the stars must be giant globes of fire like our Sun. The idea was so simple that he could not believe no one had thought of it before. Copernicus was, however, a deeply religious man. He knew that to question the geocentric theory that the Catholic Church supported was considered a great sin. Despite his spiritual conflicts, however, he could not help but continue his research.

In the early 1530s, Copernicus wrote of his findings in the first draft of a book called *The Revolution of the Heavenly Orbs.*

While Copernicus still had doubts about some of his ideas, word of his discoveries spread across Europe. Church leaders began to attack Copernicus. Rather than question the doctrine of the Catholic Church, Copernicus checked and rechecked his calculations. His book remained unpublished.

In 1539, a young professor named Georg Joachim Rheticus came to see the aging Copernicus. Rheticus begged the astronomer to publish *The Revolution of the Heavenly Orbs*. Finally in 1543, Copernicus allowed the book to be published.

Copernicus's book caused an uproar. Its findings basically contradicted the very creation principles of the Holy Bible. It removed Earth from the center of the universe. Copernicus had set the world in motion.

In 1616, the Catholic Church placed *The Revolution of the Heavenly Orbs* on its list of banned books. It stayed there for over 200 years. Before it was banned, however, it fell into the hands of another stargazer. He was a German math teacher who eventually proved Copernicus wrong—not about Earth moving around the Sun, but in the mathematical methods used to prove the theory.

Kepler the Mathematician

Johannes Kepler, born in 1571, disputed the theories put forth by Copernicus. Like Copernicus, Kepler was a religious man. Kepler believed that if he could better understand the universe, he could better understand God.

Before Kepler could start, however, he had to solve some Earth-bound problems. He needed highly accurate instruments to observe the planets. Kepler knew of a legendary astronomer who lived in Denmark. Tycho Brahe was a nobleman who was known far and wide as one of the greatest instrument makers in the world. These instruments helped Brahe measure the stars. Brahe had dozens of journals filled with his star maps. But Kepler did not have enough money to travel all the way from Germany to Denmark.

Brahe moved to Prague, Czechoslovakia, in 1599. He was made the Imperial Mathematician in the court of the Holy Roman Emperor Rudolph II. Kepler decided to make the trip to Prague to ask Brahe to share his data. Kepler visited Brahe, who offered him a job: He was to calculate the orbit of Mars. Kepler began work on this difficult problem, one that had frustrated many astronomers before him.

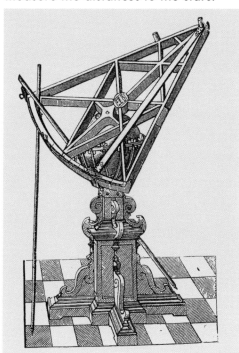

Tycho Brahe invented an instrument called an astronomical sextant to measure the distances to the stars.

On October 24, 1601, the great astronomer Brahe died. Kepler was offered his job as Imperial Mathematician. Kepler worked on the problem of Mars for over five years. After filling 900 pages in a book with his calculations, he still couldn't predict the planet's orbit. As a last resort, nearly ready to quit, Kepler drew an oval, or elliptical, orbit instead of a circular one. That was it! Mars moved in an ellipse, not in a circle. In a single defining moment, Kepler had solved a problem that had confounded astronomers for many centuries.

Using the notion that Mars moved in an ellipse, Kepler set out to plot the motion of the other planets. Over the years, he discovered three laws that ruled the motion of planets. They were eventually called Kepler's Laws of Planetary Motion.

The first law states that the Sun is not at the center of a planet's orbit, but is offset slightly in an ellipse. The second law states that a planet moves faster when closer to the Sun and slower when farther away. Kepler's third law states that the inner planets move faster around the Sun than the outer planets.

Although Kepler observed these laws, he did not understand *why* they existed. How did planets know where in their orbits to speed up or slow down? Did an invisible force come from the Sun to control the planets? Kepler didn't know. But before long, someone else would provide more answers.

Galileo's Telescope

Galileo Galilei was an Italian scientist born in 1564. By the time he was 45 years old, he had studied medicine, math, and mechanics. In 1609, Galileo obtained some glass lenses from a Dutch optician and put them into a long wooden tube. One lens was concave—arched in towards the center. The other was convex—arched outward. Galileo put the lenses in the simple telescope and when he pointed it at a nearby building, the building looked three times closer.

People had been using very simple telescopes on ships for some time. But Galileo saw another value in the telescope. After experimenting with several lenses, he soon had built the most powerful telescope in the world. Galileo put the

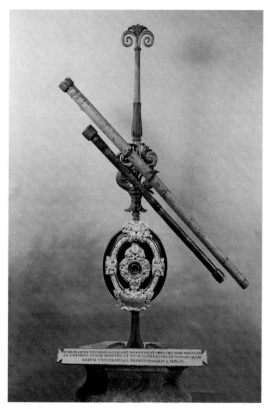
Galileo invented this powerful telescope to observe the planets and stars.

instrument on a stand and pointed it at the Moon, which was setting in the sky. The Moon appeared 30 times closer. Through his telescope, the Moon didn't look anything like the smooth, perfectly round globe others had described. It was pock-marked with holes and its surface was cracked and splintered. Galileo also saw mountains that he thought to be 4 miles (6.4 kilometers) high. (Galileo's estimates were pretty close—the highest peaks on the Moon rise about 3 miles [4.8 kilometers] above the surface.)

Galileo also aimed his telescope at the stars, and could see thousands of them never seen before by the human eye. He thought that the stars must be very far away from Earth if they still looked like such small points of light. He watched the heavens night after night and made dozens of sketches in his journal.

On January 7, 1610, Galileo saw the bright planet Jupiter glowing in the sky. When he peered through his telescope he noticed three stars nearby—two in the east, one in the west. The next night when he looked at Jupiter, the three tiny stars had moved. Now they were all west of the planet. A few nights later, Galileo saw only two points of light near Jupiter. After 13 nights, the scientist saw four stars around Jupiter—one in the east and three in the west. Finally Galileo realized that these weren't stars at all, but moons. To Galileo, this proved that Copernicus was right. Earth could not be the center of all things. He described the four moons and Jupiter as a miniature model of our solar system to illustrate his point.

Galileo published his exciting findings in March 1610, in a short book called *The Starry Messenger*. The book caused quite a stir in Europe—once again angering the Roman Catholic Church with its implications—and was read as far away as China.

When he wasn't gazing at the night sky, Galileo conducted other experiments to study how our universe worked. In one, he proved that in the absence of air, all falling objects behave the same, no matter what their size or weight. In other words, any two objects dropped in a vacuum will fall at the same rate. The famous English physicist Isaac Newton would later use this knowledge to develop his laws of motion.

Newton Pulls the World Together

Isaac Newton was born on Christmas Day in 1642 (the same year as Galileo's death), in Woolsthorpe, England. As an adult, Newton completed the revolution begun by Copernicus a century before.

Newton asked many questions about the universe. Why did the planets circle the Sun rather than fly off into space? Why did an apple fall straight down when it fell off a tree instead of landing many feet, or even miles, away? Newton theorized that a mysterious force must be coming from the center of Earth and that it kept everything from flying off into space.

The Trials of Galileo

Galileo's book, *The Starry Messenger*, proved Copernicus's theory that the Sun was the center of our solar system. When the Catholic Church became angry, Galileo went to Rome to try and make peace.

On February 16, 1616, the Church ordered Galileo to stop defending the "false" doctrine of a spinning Earth orbiting the Sun. Worried and tired, Galileo went home and kept to himself. In 1624, he decided to write a book about the two conflicting schools of thought—Earth-centered versus Sun-centered. The book, called *Dialogue Concerning the Two Chief World Systems*, was not published until 1632. But when it was, all the copies printed sold in a short time. When Church officials saw the book, Galileo was brought to Rome and ordered to stand trial. Others had been burned at the stake for questioning the Church's teachings, so Galileo was fearful.

In 1633, Galileo was found guilty of heresy, which means holding beliefs contrary to Church doctrine. He was forced to kneel before the court and state that Earth was the center of the universe. He was then placed under house arrest, where he remained until he died. Some records indicate that, as he walked from the courtroom, Galileo was heard to mutter, "...and still the Earth moves." Galileo died in 1642. He wasn't officially forgiven by the Catholic Church until 1992—more than 350 years after his conviction.

He reasoned that it must be the same force that holds planets in their orbits.

For the next several years, Newton studied Kepler's Laws of Planetary Motion. Newton decided that space was held together by an invisible force that he named gravity. Gravity came from the centers of all heavenly bodies and pulled all things toward them. He reasoned that the larger an object was, the stronger its pull of gravity would be.

Newton invented a powerful new form of math called calculus that he used to prove theories put forth by Brahe and Kepler. As he worked on these theories, which now form the foundation of modern physics, Newton discovered a set of laws about motion. The first law describes inertia. That is, any object not moving will stand still unless it is affected by an outside force. If the object is moving, it will continue to move at a constant speed in a straight line. The second law states that when a force causes a change in the speed of an object, the rate of change is in proportion to the strength of that force.

Newton explained his laws using an apple and a pebble launched from a slingshot. An apple, affected only by gravity, falls to the ground in a straight line that would pass through the center of Earth. A pebble flying from a sling-shot is affected by the force of the slingshot *and* gravity. The pebble follows a straight path even as gravity pulls it toward Earth. The force of the launch determines how far it will travel. The strength of Earth's gravity determines how quickly the pebble will be pulled toward Earth once it stops flying.

Newton reasoned that if a pebble was launched with enough force, it would travel around Earth and hit

Newton's laws of motion supported his theories about the way planets orbit the Sun—theories that stand unquestioned today.

the shooter in the back of the head. If the shooter ducked, the pebble would orbit forever. Newton knew that Earth's atmosphere would prevent such a thing from really happening, but he used the theory to explain why the Moon orbits Earth.

Captured by Earth's gravity, the Moon—a satellite of Earth—is always falling toward our planet. But its horizontal speed keeps it going around endlessly. The same laws apply to other planets and their satellites and to the solar system as a whole.

Newton arrived at his theories using a process called thought experimentation. He used an imaginary scene—the apple and the pebble—to discover laws that governed the real world. This method is now used by scientists all over the world. It is especially useful to cosmologists—scientists who study the universe—whose theories are not always possible to test.

Isaac Newton's work showed mathematical proof that established the paths of the planets and comets around the Sun. It also proved that ocean tides are caused by gravity. Newton even discovered a way to launch human-made satellites into orbit—270 years before that ever became a reality.

After Isaac

Newton's theories of motion worked very well. They could explain a planet moving through the night sky or a ball shot from a cannon. In 1846, using Newton's laws of motion and gravity, two mathematicians predicted that there was a large planet beyond Uranus. In September, they discovered the planet Neptune.

By the later half of the nineteenth century, physicists worked on other cosmic problems—most notably, how electricity and magnetism were related to how energy travels through space.

It was known that electricity could move a magnetic compass needle and a moving magnet could produce an electrical current through wire. Then in 1865, a Scottish physicist named James Clerk Maxwell described the relationship between electricity and magnetism. Maxwell's equations showed that electricity moved in waves, like those caused by a pebble tossed in a pond. He said that electric waves moved at the same speed as light, which had already been discovered to be about 186,000 miles (299,000 kilometers) per second. Maxwell concluded that electromagnetic waves were the same as light waves. He wrote that visible light was only one form of electromagnetic energy. The only difference, he theorized, was in the length of the waves.

An artist's illustration depicts a U.S. spacecraft in orbit above Neptune in 1989—more than 140 years after the planet was discovered.

As the century drew to a close, many great cosmic questions had been answered. The distances to the stars had been measured in light-years. The stars and planets had been photographed. And the Milky Way was determined to be 100,000 light-years in diameter, and 10,000 light-years thick. What new discoveries could still be made? Answers were brewing in the mind of a young man named Albert Einstein.

Albert Einstein's theories would forever change the way scientists thought about how the universe works.

CHAPTER 2

IT'S ALL RELATIVE: DR. EINSTEIN'S UNIVERSE

In 1895, a 16-year-old high-school dropout was walking through the hills of northern Italy. As he approached the town of Pavia, the long-haired boy noticed sunbeams glistening on a lake, bouncing off a stream, and reflecting on a snowy mountain top. The young man, Albert Einstein, wondered what the world would look like if he could ride on a beam of light. At the time, it was a question no one had been able to answer. But young Einstein spent much of his time asking himself "what if...?" and asking others probing questions about the hows and whys of the universe that had not yet been answered.

E = mc²: The Theory of Relativity

In 1905, Einstein published the first in a series of articles in a scientific journal called the *Annals of Physics*. He focused on the question that had fascinated him earlier in life: What would it be like to ride on a beam of light?

In an article called "On the Electrodynamics of Moving Bodies," Einstein introduced a theory that later became known as the special theory of relativity. In later years, this theory would lead Einstein to his famous general theory of relativity.

The special theory defied common sense and ordinary human experience. It also extended Newton's laws. Newton had written that "Absolute, true, and mathematical time…flows equally without relation to anything external." But Einstein's research led him to believe that time *did* depend on something else and that time did *not* flow equally, or at a constant rate. He proposed that time was always relative to the person observing it.

This may be proven by the following thought experiment. Imagine that you heard a horn blow at the exact moment you walked out of your house. The sound came from some distance away and took an interval of time to travel to where you, the observer, were standing. Therefore, the horn blast and your exit were not *exactly* simultaneous. That means that determining whether or not two things happened at the same time depends on speed (velocity), time, and the position of the observer.

Consider also that the measurement of an hour is relative to the observer. It can seem like a long time when he or she is doing something boring. Or it can seem like a very short time when he or she is doing something exciting.

The Theory of Uniform Motion

One principle of the special theory is that most measurements are not absolute or fixed. Instead, they depend on the motions of their measurers—especially at speeds approaching the speed of light. A simplified version of the theory may be demonstrated by observers traveling at a steady speed in a straight line—what physicists call uniform motion. To a girl standing still, a passing schoolbus is in uniform motion moving away from her. To a person on the bus, the girl and the field appear to be in motion heading the other way.

A physicist might say that the bus and the field represent two different "frames of reference." Observers inside a uniformly

Frame of Reference

To an observer standing still, a ball dropped by a motorcyclist traveling at a steady speed will appear to fall in an arc. The motorcyclist, however, will see the ball drop straight down. The observer and the motorcyclist perceive the ball dropping from two different frames of reference.

Einstein as a World Citizen

Albert Einstein was one of the twentieth century's most important scientists. In 1921, he won the Nobel Prize in physics. Photographers and reporters followed him wherever he traveled. He regretted his loss of privacy, but used his fame to further his own political and social views.

Einstein's most strongly held beliefs were pacifism and Zionism. Pacifism is opposition to all war and violence. Zionism is a world-wide Jewish movement that led to the establishment of the modern state of Israel. During World War I, Einstein was one of a group of German scientists who opposed Germany's involvement in the war. After the war, his continued public support of pacifist and Zionist goals made him a target of vicious attacks within Germany. Even his scientific theories were publicly ridiculed—especially the theory of relativity.

When Adolf Hitler and the Nazis came to power in Germany in 1933, Einstein left the country. He took a position at the Institute for Advanced Study in Princeton, New Jersey. Einstein temporarily put aside his pacifist views in the face of the threat Nazi Germany posed to all of humankind. In 1939, Einstein wrote a letter to President Franklin D. Roosevelt pointing out that the Nazis were probably working on an atom bomb. Einstein suggested that the president begin working on a plan to defend America against nuclear threat. His theories were used by other scientists in the

moving frame will find physical events inside that frame unaffected by its motion. If the windows were covered, a person on a bus that was moving extremely smoothly and at a constant velocity might not feel as if he or she were moving at all.

When a person looks outside their frame, their motion *relative* to another frame is what they see. This difference

After leaving Nazi Germany in 1933, Einstein became a U.S. citizen. Here, he takes the citizenship oath in 1940.

creation of the atomic bomb. After the war, Einstein became active in the cause of international disarmament and world government.

Einstein died in Princeton, New Jersey, on April 18, 1955. Although he gave much of himself to political and social causes, science was his first love.

in perception is the result of relativity's other principle: Every observer perceives light as traveling through space at the same speed. The beam of a headlight on a moving bus travels at the same speed as a beam of light from a stationary flashlight.

And because light has a given speed, it takes a certain amount of time to travel *to* the observer. Thus, two observers traveling at separate speeds will receive the light and record the information at separate times. The outcome is that observers in different frames of reference will have different *perceptions* of the time it took for the light to travel. In addition, an observer *of* a moving object and a traveler *in* the moving object have different perceptions of the properties of that object.

To demonstrate this, imagine an astronaut riding in a space shuttle traveling close to the speed of light. To the astronaut onboard, time, and the mass, size, and shape of objects remain constant. To an observer on Earth, the space shuttle appears to

Time and Space Travel

As illustrated, to an observer on Earth, the dimensions of a space shuttle would appear to change as it approached the speed of light. But to the astronaut onboard the space shuttle, everything would remain constant.

be changing as the speed increases. The mass increases toward infinite, the length approaches zero, and time appears to stop. This theory has been used in science-fiction stories where astronauts traveling at the speed of light did not age in relation to people who remain on Earth.

According to Einstein's theory, there is no absolute measurement of time, space, or motion. The height, width, and length of an object and the length of an event are not fixed values. They may only be determined by the motion of the observer's frame of reference. Light is constant; space and time are relative.

Building on this theory, Einstein used simple algebra to extend his assumptions. He was able to show that when an object moves at speeds close to the speed of light, its mass (the amount of stuff something is made of) increases in proportion to its kinetic energy (the energy caused by its motion). From this relationship between mass and energy, he deduced that the two are equal. He expressed this in the equation $E = mc^2$, where E is the energy content of an object, m is its mass, and c is the speed of light.

Einstein knew his theory defied common sense, but believed that the laws of the universe were not designed to satisfy human senses. The theory also showed that matter was simply an extremely concentrated form of energy. Under the right conditions, huge amounts of energy could be released from tiny bits of matter. If a certain type of atom—the smallest particle of a chemical element—is bombarded with a very large amount of radioactive energy, a nuclear reaction will result. This is how Einstein's theory was later used by other scientists to develop the atom bomb.

The Pull of Gravity

When Einstein's theories were published, he was praised by the world's most famous scientists. By 1919, Einstein himself was world famous. By this time, he had been working on relativity for almost 14 years. Einstein wanted to broaden the scope of his theory to include objects that were moving in a non-uniform way. To do that, he examined the relationship between acceleration produced by gravity and that generated by other forces.

Einstein imagined a person in a room traveling through space at a constant speed. The person in the room would be weightless, floating freely. There would be no up or down, no floor or ceiling. But if a constant force were applied to one side of the room, the person would accelerate uniformly. The force would feel just like the force of gravity felt by someone on Earth. The person inside would not know if the force were due to acceleration or gravity. Therefore, Einstein said, gravity and acceleration are equal. This is called the principle of equivalence.

If the motions of gravity and acceleration are equal then their measurements are also subject to the special theory. Einstein said that a clock subject to the force of gravity runs faster than one farther away from gravity's force. This was proven in the 1960s by researchers using extremely accurate atomic clocks. Clocks in Denver, Colorado—5,280 feet (1,610 meters) above sea level—gained about fifteen-billionths of a second per day over clocks in Washington, D.C.—near sea level. Other experiments showed that an atomic clock on the ground floor of a building ran more slowly than one 74 feet (23 meters) above it.

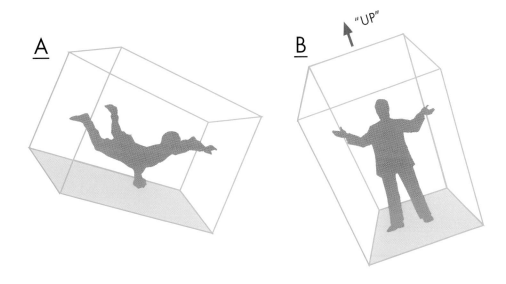

The Principle of Equivalence

Figure A shows a person in a box traveling at a constant speed through space with no force exerted upon him; therefore he is weightless. Figure B shows a person in a box that has a constant force applied to it. This box now accelerates uniformly and has an "up." This uniform acceleration in space has the same effect as gravity on Earth.

Gravity Wells and the Fabric of Space

While developing the principle of equivalence, Einstein used mathematics to define the interactions between matter, radiation, and gravitational forces. These equations were so complex that they stretched Einstein's abilities to the near breaking point. At one point he wrote to his friend Marcel Grossman, "Help me Marcel, or I'll go crazy!" Grossman introduced Einstein to a different kind of geometry developed during the nineteenth century by Bernhard Reimann. Traditional geometry, called

How to Become a Cosmologist

Cosmology is defined as the study of the origin and structure of the universe. To become a cosmologist, one must first become a physicist. The study of physics can be divided into two fields—theoretical and experimental. Experimental physicists take measurements and make observations. They use complicated equipment like particle accelerators, radio telescopes, and high-intensity lasers. Theoretical physicists, like Albert Einstein and Stephen Hawking, find patterns in data obtained by experimental physicists. Using these patterns, theoretical physicists begin to understand different processes and make predictions.

Anyone planning a career in physics must have a strong math background. Books written by Einstein explaining the general theory of relativity contain page after page of complicated mathematical formulas. Algebra, calculus, geometry, and trigonometry are all subjects studied by cosmologists. Other subjects cosmologists should excel in are the computer sciences, astronomy, and basic engineering. Latin, philosophy, and religion also add to a cosmologist's expertise.

A cosmologist should always be willing to search for new answers. Scientists like Einstein are never satisfied with simple answers. Even when they solve one problem, they keep looking further. What is the next question that lies behind the last answer? With talent, education, and creative minds, cosmologists tackle some of the most elusive questions of our world.

Euclidean geometry after its Greek inventor, used straight lines. Non-Euclidean geometry worked with curved surfaces and spaces. This geometry helped Einstein define his theory of general relativity.

General relativity was meant to provide one explanation for all physical events. This included the way a light beam travels the shortest path between two points. In Euclidean geometry, this is a straight line, not a curved one. Using non-Euclidean geometry, Einstein described a new way of looking at the universe. Instead of light rays curving, it was the very fabric of space that was warped by gravity's pull. The theory stated that any massive object would, by its gravitational pull, bend the path of anything passing near it. This was in keeping with the curved paths of the planets orbiting around the Sun. But Einstein predicted that gravity would also bend the paths of electromagnetic waves, which include light waves. He said that a light beam, for example, would curve as it passed near a star.

General relativity also describes the universe in four dimensions. Three dimensions are in space—height, width, and length. The fourth dimension is time. Gravity is a geometrical property of four-dimensional space-time.

A way to think of this is to imagine space as a tight, stretched rubber sheet. Where there is little mass, say an asteroid, the sheet is flat. But where there are massive bodies such as stars and planets, the sheet is deformed. As stars and planets press into the sheet from above and below they make bumps, dips, and ripples called gravity wells.

Objects traveling through the universe will fall into these gravity wells. A comet, for example, moving toward a star will fall into the star's gravity well. The fall may change the comet's original path. The theory of general relativity says that bodies like a comet are not pulled in by the star's gravity. Rather they are following the warped contours of space-time itself.

According to the theory of general relativity, space—seen here as a grid in this artist's illustration—has bumps or dips called gravity wells caused by massive bodies such as stars and planets.

Einstein decided to prove his general theory by predicting the bending of starlight by the Sun's gravity well. This could only be proven during a solar eclipse. During an eclipse, a group of stars behind the Sun could be seen. The positions of the stars could be photographed and recorded. If Einstein was right, the bending of the stars' light by the Sun's gravity well would make them appear to be in a different place than their true positions in the sky.

Several expeditions were mounted to prove—or disprove—Einstein's theory. Rain obscured an Argentinean eclipse in 1912 and a German scientific expedition was canceled at the outbreak of World War I in 1914. But on May 29, 1919, an eclipse was observed as the Sun passed in front of a rich cluster of stars called the Hyades. Two groups of astronomers recorded the eclipse—one in Africa, the other in Brazil. When the photographs were developed, Einstein was proved right. The view of the stars from Earth was shifted by the warped fabric of space around the Sun. The stars appeared to be located elsewhere than their true positions in space. Concrete proof of Einstein's theory suddenly made him even more famous. Little affected by his celebrity status, Einstein continued to explore the effects of general relativity upon the universe as a whole.

The Expanding Universe

Einstein still believed many commonly held assumptions about the universe. For instance, physicists had long believed that the universe had no beginning and no end—no boundaries. They also thought the universe did not move—it was static.

Its moving parts did not fly apart or crash together, and its size did not change over time. All places in the universe were believed to be alike. No part was identical to any other part, but the overall makeup of the universe looked the same everywhere. Physicists believed that the stars we see in the sky looked about the same whether we were on Earth or somewhere else in the universe.

Using non-Euclidean geometry, Einstein proposed another theory about the boundless universe. Again defying common sense, Einstein said the universe was *curved* in four dimensional space-time. Einstein said the universe was simultaneously finite (limited) and boundless.

In trying to prove his theory, Einstein began to travel what he described as "a rough and winding road." This work involved complex mathematical calculations. Two other physicists, Willem de Sitter and Alexander Friedmann, worked on theories and calculations that they shared with Einstein.

Einstein's equations showed Friedmann that there could be a wide variety of ways the universe might work. Friedmann was fascinated by Einstein's work and the mathematical challenges it presented. Friedmann's results showed matter-filled expanding universes. He divided these into two classes. In one of his models, the universe would continue to expand forever. In another, it would expand until the gravitational attraction of matter caused the universe to collapse on itself.

Friedmann's work was published in 1922. Einstein read the paper, and wrote his own paper to disprove Friedmann's work. But within a year, Einstein changed his mind. Although he then believed the math to be correct, Einstein could still see

In 1931, Willem de Sitter and Einstein worked together on calculations that attempted to help explain the structure of the universe.

no practical use for Friedmann's theories. It would be another few years before astronomers would discover how relativity would drastically affect our understanding of the universe.

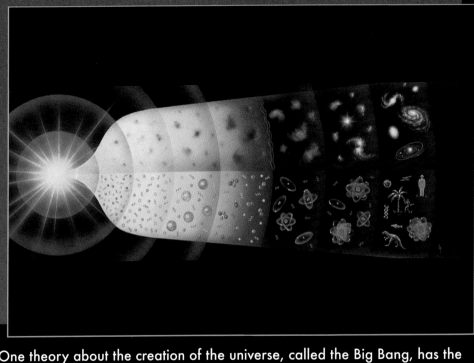

One theory about the creation of the universe, called the Big Bang, has the universe and its contents originating from a single, cataclysmic explosion, which released a tremendous amount of energy. Here, an artist's conception of the Big Bang shows particles changing over billions of years to form galaxies, planets, and animal and human life.

CHAPTER 3

BIG BANG TO BIG CRUNCH?

In the 1920s, astronomers were still trying to make Einstein's general theory of relativity fit into the observable universe. Different solutions to Einstein's equations seemed to allow different types of universes to exist at the same time. It seemed that the universe could be either expanding or contracting, empty or filled with matter. None of the models seemed to describe the universe as people on Earth observed it—stationary and lightly populated with stars. Before the solution to the problem could be found, new insights into the atom and energy were necessary. And the new language of quantum mechanics would have to be invented.

The Big Bang Theory

One of the first people to describe the creation of the universe in scientific terms was a Belgian Catholic priest who was also a physicist. Georges Lemaître was ordained as a priest in 1923. At the time, he was also studying to become a theoretical physicist.

Lemaître learned that there were distant galaxies that were moving away from our Milky Way galaxy at speeds of 700 miles (1,126 kilometers) per second. In 1927, Lemaître published mathematical models that showed that the universe was a constant mass that increased without limit at speeds matching those of distant galaxies. Although he didn't know it, his calculations were amazingly close to those published by Friedmann in 1922. But while Friedmann had treated the problem as a mathematical experiment, Lemaître connected the math to actual observations of astronomy. This was the first time the principles of relativity had been connected to the observable universe. Like Friedmann's work, however, Lemaître's calculations went largely unnoticed for several years.

Meanwhile, Lemaître turned his attention to other problems. He did a thought experiment in which he imagined a moving image of the expanding universe—in reverse. Instead of the galaxies moving apart at hundreds of miles per second, Lemaître imagined them moving together. Space shrank and the distances between the galaxies became miles instead of light-years.

In 1927, Lemaître first proposed that there might be a real beginning of time and space. Before expansion got under way,

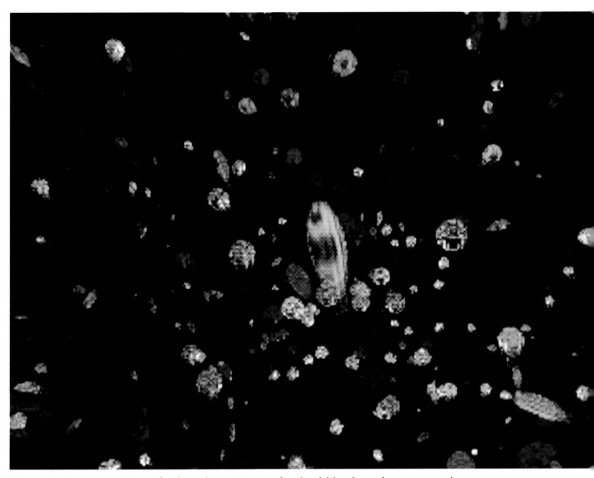

An artist's conception of what the universe looked like less than one millionth of a second after the Big Bang shows particles that make up atoms.

a "primeval atom" existed. This atom weighed as much as the entire universe. Within the atom, electrical forces of positive and negative atoms did not exist. Matter was extremely hot and compressed. Next, Lemaître speculated this "cosmic egg" flung its contents out with an enormous explosion. Following this "Big Bang," the universe underwent a slow expansion and evolution that accounted for the next 2 billion years.

Women Physicists

In the last century, there have been many women who have contributed significantly to the study of our universe.

In the late 1800s, Sonya Kovalevski, a Russian mathematician, devised a formula to analyze the rings of Saturn. Amazingly, she learned calculus by staring at the walls of her bedroom, which were papered with copies of lectures on calculus. At the age of 18, Kovalevski went to Germany to further her education. In 1888, she won the prestigious prize from the French Academy of Sciences for her paper on the rotation of a solid body around a fixed point.

Another important female physicist was Emmy Noether. Noether was born in Germany in 1882. Although not allowed to formally attend a university, she observed math classes at the University of Erlangen. After German women were given the right to vote in 1904, Noether was also able to enroll in the university and received a doctorate with highest honors in 1907. In 1919, she officially joined the faculty at the University of Göttingen. In 1922, Noether began to work with Albert Einstein.

Einstein needed some new math terms to express his theory of general relativity. Noether provided some of the mathematical

Lemaître's vision relied on the principles of relativity to describe vast distances and large masses. Relativity allowed him to describe mathematically the expansion as originating from a very small source. It did not allow him, however, to understand the physical properties of his "primeval atom." Such a tiny, dense lump of matter was hard to imagine when looking at the distant galaxies. What was needed was a mathematical language that could describe the very small.

language for him. She also helped construct a formula called Noether's theorem, which is used in quantum mechanics. During World War II, Noether, who was Jewish, fled Nazi Germany and went to America. She taught at Bryn Mawr College in Pennsylvania, and began lecturing at the Institute of Advanced Study in Princeton, New Jersey, where Einstein had also gone. After her death in 1935, Einstein called Noether "the most significant creative mathematical genius thus far produced since the higher education of women began."

One of the most famous female astrophysicists is Sally Kristen Ride. Ride became an astrophysicist in 1978 and entered the U.S. space program. After competing against 8,000 other applicants, Ride was chosen to be the first American woman to travel into space. On June 18, 1983, Ride blasted off in the space shuttle *Challenger*. She made a second space flight in 1984. When the tragic explosion of the *Challenger* occurred in 1986, Ride became a member of the presidential commission that was to investigate the causes of the accident. In 1989, Ride became a professor of physics and director of the California Space Institute at the University of California at San Diego.

How Is Our Universe Structured?

By the end of the 1930s, physicists had put together two schools of thought for analyzing the universe. One was on a large scale—planets, stars, and galaxies. The other was on a very small, subatomic scale. Physicists understood the atom to be made up of charged electrons surrounding a nucleus. The nucleus was made up of protons and neutrons. These tiny

The Structure of the Universe

Three major theories about the possible structure of our universe are as follows:

Open universe

1) An open universe that began with the Big Bang and continues in a gradual expansion.

Flat universe

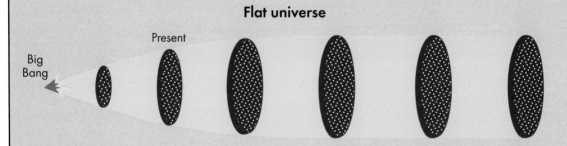

2) A flat universe that began with the Big Bang and was followed by an expansion that stays constant.

Closed universe

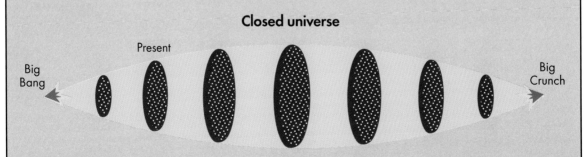

3) A closed universe that began with the Big Bang, followed by an expansion and eventually a contraction, ending one day in a Big Crunch.

particles were governed by rules quite different from the rules of the world at large. The math created to study the world of subatomic particles was called quantum mechanics.

Both the origin and the future of the universe depend on how dense it is. The denser the universe, the bigger its gravitational force. Scientists have come up with many theories on the structure and fate of our universe. Among them are three theories that have received a lot of attention. They are the open, flat, and closed universe theories. All three of these begin with the Big Bang. The open universe theory says that following the Big Bang there was a gradual expansion that is still occurring. The flat universe theory states that there was an expansion after the Big Bang that stabilized and the universe remains a constant size. The closed universe theory proposes that the gradual expansion will eventually become a contraction, resulting in a Big Crunch—the ultimate collapse of the universe.

Stephen Hawking and the History of Time

Stephen Hawking, a brilliant British physicist, used quantum mechanics to search for answers about the universe. He was the first person to combine quantum theory with general relativity. In the early 1970s, Hawking worked with the two theories to learn about the origin of the universe. The two theories combined were called quantum gravity.

As the years passed, Hawking became convinced that there might not have been one Big Bang, one single moment of creation. He believed the effects of quantum gravity indicated this.

Stephen Hawking: Working with Disabilities

Stephen Hawking was born exactly 300 years after the death of Galileo. In 1963, soon after he turned 21 years old, Hawking was told that he had amyotrophic lateral sclerosis (ALS) and had only two years to live. Today, well past the age of 50, Hawking continues to defy the odds and live with ALS. Hawking was confined to a wheelchair in 1972. But he challenged each phase of the disease. When he could no longer walk, he pulled himself up a steep flight of stairs to go to bed every night using only the strength of his arms.

In 1974, Hawking became a member of the Royal Society of Great Britain. For 300 years, its members had included only the best British scientists. Hawking—at the time 32 years old—was the youngest person ever admitted. He was so weak that he could barely sign the Society's roll book, but he managed to write his name in the same book that Isaac Newton had once signed. It was the last time Hawking would ever be able to write his name.

In 1985, Hawking got pneumonia. This is the cause of death for many ALS victims. Unable to breathe, Hawking's doctors opened a passage for air in his throat. This caused him to lose his ability to speak. Walt Woltosz, a computer software developer in California, gave Hawking a program he had created called Equalizer. The program runs on a small computer attached to Hawking's wheelchair. Hawking can only move a few of his fingers, but by using a clicker he can choose from among 3,000 words. When a word is not in the program's vocabulary, Hawking can use the clicker to spell out the word he needs. The computer is attached to a voice synthesizer also mounted on the wheelchair that gives voice to the words he chooses. In this way, Hawking has continued to communicate his brilliant gifts of scientific understanding to the world.

He reasoned that this also showed that there may not be a Big Crunch in the future. If the universe did not begin with one explosion, he proposed, then it would not end with one either.

In 1988, Hawking published a best-selling book called *A Brief History of Time*. In it, he suggests that the universe had no beginning and has no end. He pictures it as a complete structure, closing back on itself smoothly in time and in space. Each expansion leads to a new contraction.

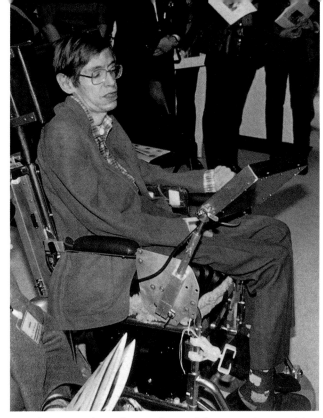

Stephen Hawking has achieved fame in the world of physics and cosmology for developing startling theories about the origins of the universe.

This theory made some people uneasy. If the universe had no beginning and has no end, they reasoned, then there is no moment of creation. This is a notion that can be very upsetting to people who believe in creation—and a creator. "What place then," asks Hawking, "for a creator?" His thoughts: "If we do discover a complete theory of the universe, it should, in time be understandable . . . by everyone, not just a few scientists. Then we shall all, philosophers, scientists, and just ordinary people, be able to take part in . . . why it is that we and the universe exist. If we find the answer to that, it would be the ultimate triumph of human reason—for then we would know the mind of God."

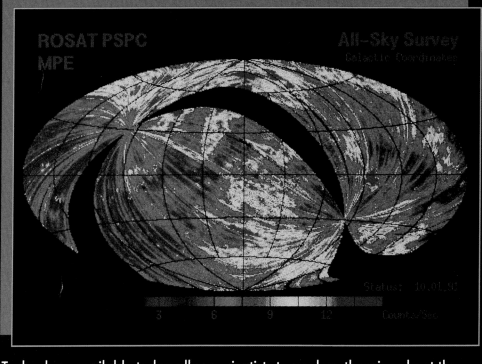

ROSAT PSPC
MPE

All-Sky Survey
Galactic Coordinates

Status: 10.01.90

3   6   9   12   Counts/Sec

Technology available today allows scientists to explore theories about the
origins of the universe. Here, an x-ray picture of our galaxy taken by an
astronomical satellite shows colors that represent different intensities of
radiation.

CHAPTER 4

THE ENDS OF THE UNIVERSE

When it was first proposed, the theory of relativity was just that—a theory. There was little technology available to prove Einstein right or wrong. At the time that Einstein was talking about light beams, the automobile and the airplane had only recently been invented. Trains were about the fastest thing on Earth, moving passengers at speeds under 60 miles (96 kilometers) per hour. There was no such thing as a hand-held calculator. Television and computers were just dreams of the future. Einstein died 14 years before men ever walked on the Moon. But as technology advanced, Einstein's theories were scientifically proven.

The same situation could be said to exist regarding today's theories of the universe. The Big Bang and the Big Crunch are still theories that have not been completely proven.

Echo of the Big Bang

In 1965, Robert Wilson (at left) and Arno Penzias (at right) discovered microwave radiation left over from the Big Bang.

During the 1940s and 1950s, debate raged over Lemaître's Big Bang theories. Physicists who believed in the Big Bang thought that some trace of the explosion could still be found in deep space. They reasoned that intense microwave radiation would have survived the cosmic fireball. In fact, they believed the leftover radiation should be everywhere in space. In 1965, evidence of the Big Bang turned up in an unexpected place.

Two researchers for Bell Laboratories, Arno Penzias and Robert Wilson, were looking for a way to relay telephone calls through communications satellites in space. They used huge microwave antennas for this purpose. Problems arose when the researchers found unexpected microwave interference coming from space. The signals gave off a uniform intensity in every region of the sky the researchers checked. It was microwave radiation, and it was the answer cosmologists were looking for. These microwaves were the earliest traces of the Big Bang.

While scientists were studying microwaves in the mid-1960s, computer technology was quickly improving. Although primitive by today's standards, these early computers helped to put pieces of the universal puzzle into place.

New Dimensions: Computers and the Cosmos

As recently as 1950, most of the information about the cosmos came from the visual light it emitted. Today, astronomers can study not only light waves but all types of radiation released from celestial bodies in the universe. This includes X rays, radio waves, gamma rays, and infrared and ultraviolet light. Every object emits electromagnetic fields that are measured in wavelengths. Hot sources radiate at shorter wavelengths than cool ones. For instance, super-heated gases from exploding stars release X rays that have wavelengths of only a millionth of a centimeter, while cool, dark clouds of gas emit radio signals with wavelengths as long as 4 inches (10 centimeters).

To gather and analyze this cosmic information, scientists use enormous and very sophisticated computers. Along with the study of photographs, cosmologists channel radiation into electronic detectors that create digital pictures on computer screens. The images can then be stored and even transmitted over the Internet. A technique called false-color imaging permits the addition of different colors to these digital pictures. The various colors help astronomers see patterns in the radiation they collect.

Computers have aided scientists in making major discoveries about the universe since the mid-1960s. In addition to examining the skies, computers help solve complex questions by allowing researchers to make models of stars, galaxies, and even entire universes. Programmed with the laws of mass, gravity, and motion, computers can chart the evolution of a model universe.

Scientists today use computers to examine and map our universe.

The *Cosmic Background Explorer*

In 1989, the National Aeronautics and Space Administration (NASA) launched a spacecraft called the *Cosmic Background Explorer*, or COBE. The COBE's mission was to study the microwaves left from the Big Bang. The COBE proved that the microwaves found were exactly the kind cosmologists had predicted.

The COBE sent computer pictures back to Earth so scientists would have images of the Big Bang's radiation. It also sent back dramatic pictures of the Milky Way.

The COBE is not the only satellite searching space for cosmic answers. Over the years, hundreds of research satellites have been launched—most of them from the United States and the former Soviet Union. Once free of Earth's atmosphere, satellites detect things that could never be seen from the confines of our planet.

In 1990, the Hubble Space Telescope was launched by the United States. Circling 370 miles (595 kilometers) above Earth, Hubble beams back images from 14 billion light-years away. Stars 40 times fainter than those visible from Earth can be seen by the Hubble.

As science and technology advance, humans learn more from new data and make new discoveries about the farthest reaches of space. From Galileo's telescope to supercomputers and beyond, new dimensions of space and time continue to be revealed to humankind.

A false-color image taken by COBE shows radiation remnants (red curve) from the Big Bang.

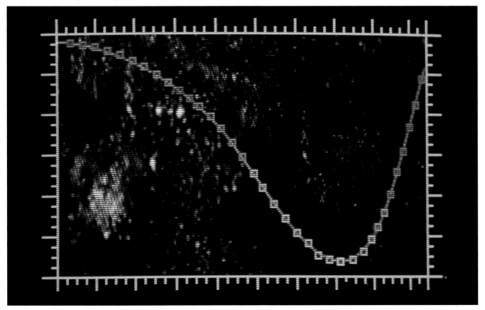

Into the Future

Some of the latest research conducted on the birth of the universe is happening in an unlikely place. Instead of looking in the sky, a group of physicists are working underground. Scientists at the U.S. Department of Energy (DOE) have built a facility 2,341 feet (725 meters) under the surface of Earth, in an abandoned iron ore mine in Tower, Minnesota. There, scientists are building a $55 million particle detector filled with argon gas that will be pointed toward Chicago, Illinois. The detector will catch tiny particles called neutrinos that may help scientists determine how the universe was created.

Four hundred and fifty miles (724 kilometers) away, scientists at Fermilab—a nuclear research facility west of Chicago—are building a $75 million underground gun to aim at the particle detector in Tower. The Fermilab gun will create vast amounts of

The Fermilab research facility conducts experiments with atomic particles in an effort to understand their role in the origin of the universe.

neutrinos. They will be shot through Earth—through the ground that runs beneath the state of Wisconsin—all the way to the detector in Minnesota. This sophisticated experiment is designed to answer some of the trickiest questions in physics about the fate of the universe.

Neutrinos are particles of energy given off when protons and electrons are combined to form neutrons. Neutrinos are the ghosts of the subatomic particle world. Every cubic centimeter of space contains about 200 of them moving at the speed of light. In spite of their high numbers, they are very difficult to detect. This is because they have no electrical charge. While neutrinos are the most common thing in the universe, they are almost impossible to capture and measure. In the time it takes to read this sentence, trillions of neutrinos will have passed right through your body. By the time you finish this paragraph, those neutrinos will have passed through the entire Earth and zipped off into deep space. We live in a sea of neutrinos generated by the Big Bang. Zillions of them are still flying around 12 to 20 billion years later. And new ones are generated in the hearts of stars and in collisions of particles.

On completion, the neutrino detector built in Tower will weigh 10,000 tons (9,070 metric tons) and will be longer than a football field. It will be able to catch and measure neutrinos fired from Fermilab. While it's hard to catch neutrinos, it's relatively easy to make them.

Physicists want to know more about neutrinos to find out what happened the instant after the Big Bang. These tiny particles also reveal what's happening inside the Sun and other stars. Scientists know neutrinos are everywhere but they don't know if they have any mass. If a neutrino has mass—even an extremely tiny bit of mass—then taken all together, neutrinos may be the most massive things in the universe.

All the neutrinos added up may be more massive than all the stars, galaxies, and dust in the cosmos combined. Since mass is related to gravity, neutrinos might ultimately play a role in how the universe is structured, and whether it will expand forever or collapse back on itself in the Big Crunch.

The machines underground in Tower and in Chicago will be able to determine if neutrinos have mass. Neutrinos come in three types—tau, electron, and muon. But physicists think that one type switches into other types. This would be like vanilla ice cream turning into chocolate ice cream. The gun in the Fermilab will fire one type of neutrino at the receiver in Tower. If those neutrinos change into another type, then scientists will have the answer to the question of whether neutrinos have mass. Only things that have mass can change that mass. It may just be that the answer to the mystery of the Big Bang will be found underground in the tiniest particles ever discovered.

Where We Fit In

The word "time" is a human invention. So too are clocks and calendars. We know that there is a difference between the past and the future, but we don't know why. We can watch a tea cup fall from a table and break, but we'll never see that tea cup pull itself together and jump back on the table. The difference between order (the unbroken tea cup) and disorder (the broken cup) is what separates the past from the future and gives a direction to time. Therefore, while we learn from the past and plan for the future, our lives really exist in the present moment.

Some physicists believe humans may one day travel through time. We may be able to go backwards to see the Big Bang or travel forward to the Big Crunch. It may not happen in our lifetimes, but someday people may travel through tunnels of time and space.

Stephen Hawking said it best when he stated: "Why does the universe go to all the trouble of existing? Does it need a creator and if so who created him? If the universe is limited in its life, how is that different from each one of us?"

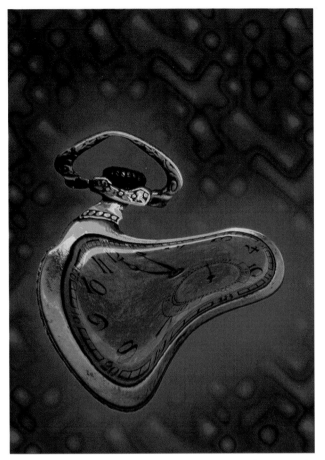

A computer illustration of a warped pocket watch depicts one aspect of the theory of general relativity: space and time are warped by gravity.

So when you look into the night sky and see stars light-years away, you can still imagine yourself at the center of the universe for a short time. No one else sees exactly what you see. No one else is in your exact time and space. And who knows? Maybe some day you may solve the riddles to the great cosmic questions. Only time will tell.

amyotrophic lateral sclerosis (ALS) A disease that slowly destroys the nerves in the brain and the spine that control the muscles.

atom The smallest particle of a chemical element.

Big Bang A theory that explains the origin and evolution of the universe, starting with a cataclysmic explosion.

Big Crunch A theory that states that the universe will collapse onto itself in the distant future after it stops expanding from the Big Bang.

black hole A region of the universe in which a very large mass is concentrated into a very small (essentially zero) volume. Scientists still disagree as to whether black holes actually exist or not.

electron A basic particle of matter, having a negative charge and existing outside the nucleus of an atom.

Euclidean geometry A branch of math that deals with points, lines, angles, and figures in space, invented by Greek mathematician Euclid.

general theory of relativity A theory developed by Albert Einstein in 1915 that attempts to explain the attraction of objects for each other in the universe.

gravity The force of attraction that exists between two bodies.

gravity well Warps in the fabric of space that are caused by massive bodies such as stars and planets.

inertia The ability of an object to remain at rest or in uniform motion.

mass The amount of material contained within an object.

Milky Way The common name for the galaxy in which our Sun and solar system are located.

non-Euclidean geometry Geometry invented by Bernhard Reimann that works with curved surfaces and spaces. Albert Einstein used non-Euclidean geometry to figure out the theory of general relativity.

principle of equivalence Albert Einstein's theory that gravity and acceleration are equal.

quantum gravity The combined use of the theory of general relativity with quantum mechanics, created by Stephen Hawking while developing theories about black holes and the origins of the universe.

quantum mechanics The branch of physics that deals with very tiny objects such as atoms and their parts.

radiation Any form of high speed particles or rays; the action of giving off energy in the form of particles or waves.

satellite A celestial or human-made object that orbits another larger body, such as a planet; the Moon is Earth's natural satellite.

speed of light The speed at which light travels: 186,000 miles (299,000 kilometers) per second.

subatomic Particles that are located inside—and are smaller than—atoms.

uniform motion The movement of an object at a constant speed in a straight line.

FURTHER READING

Asimov, Isaac. *The Birth of Our Universe.* Milwaukee: Gareth Stevens, 1995.

Branley, Franklyn. *The Sun and the Solar System.* New York: Twenty-First Century Books, 1996.

Gribbin, John. *Time & Space.* London: Dorling Kindersley, 1994.

Jaspersohn, William. *How the Universe Began.* New York: Franklin Watts, 1985.

Mammana, Dennis. *Star Hunters.* Philadelphia: Running Press, 1990.

Newton, David E. *Black Holes and Supernovae.* New York: Twenty-First Century Books, 1997.

Simon, Sheridan. *Stephen Hawking: Unlocking the Universe.* New York: Dillon Press, 1991.

ON-LINE

Albert Einstein On-Line contains information, writings, quotes, pictures, and announcements concerning the great physicist. The address is: http://www.sas.upenn.edu/~smfriedm/einstein.html

Carl Sagan was one of the world's leading cosmologists. Sagan's Science & Technology Page has a great deal of information about his work. The address is: http://www.geocities.com/Paris/4169/sagan.html For more on Carl Sagan type "Sagan, Carl" into your web search engine.

For an index of hundreds of sites concerning astronomy, browse through the Astronomical World Wide Web Resources. There are megabytes of information on everything from classes on astronomy to a who's who of famous scientists. The address is: http://www.stsci.edu/astroweb/net-www.html

SOURCES

Ancient India: The Land of Mystery. Alexandria, VA: Time-Life Books, 1994.

Asimov, Isaac. *Astronomy in Ancient Times.* Milwaukee: Gareth Stevens, 1995.

Barrow, John D. *The Origin of the Universe.* New York: Basic Books, 1994.

Clayre, Alasdair. *The Heart of the Dragon.* Boston: Houghton Mifflin, 1985.

Computers and the Cosmos. Alexandria, VA: Time-Life Books, 1988.

The Cosmos. Alexandria, VA: Time-Life Books, 1988.

Einstein, Albert. *The Meaning of Relativity.* Princeton, New Jersey: Princeton University Press, 1974.

Ferguson, Kitty. *Stephen Hawking: Quest for a Theory of the Universe.* New York: Franklin Watts, 1991.

Forsee, Aylesa. *Albert Einstein: Theoretical Physicist.* New York: Macmillan, 1967.

Ganeri, Anita. *Out of the Ark.* New York: Harcourt Brace & Company, 1996.

Hamilton, Virginia. *In the Beginning.* New York: Harcourt Brace Jovanovich, 1988.

Hawking, Stephen. *A Brief History of Time.* New York: Bantam, 1988.

Hawking, Stephen and Gene Stone. *A Brief History of Time: A Reader's Companion.* New York: Bantam, 1992.

Leeming, David and Margaret Adams Leeming. *A Dictionary of Creation Myths*. New York: Oxford University Press, 1994.

Pasachoff, Jay M. *A Field Guide to the Stars and Planets*. Boston: Houghton Mifflin, 1992.

Philip, Neil. *The Illustrated Book of Myths*. London: Dorling Kindersley, 1995.

Putnam, James. *Pyramid*. New York: Alfred A. Knopf, 1994.

Rothman, Tony. *Instant Physics*. New York: Fawcett Columbine, 1995.

Workings of the Universe. Alexandria, VA: Time-Life Books, 1988.

INDEX